A WILD CHILD'S BOOK OF BIRDS

For Mr Hill – with heartfelt thanks

~ DARA

For Juliet

~ BARRY

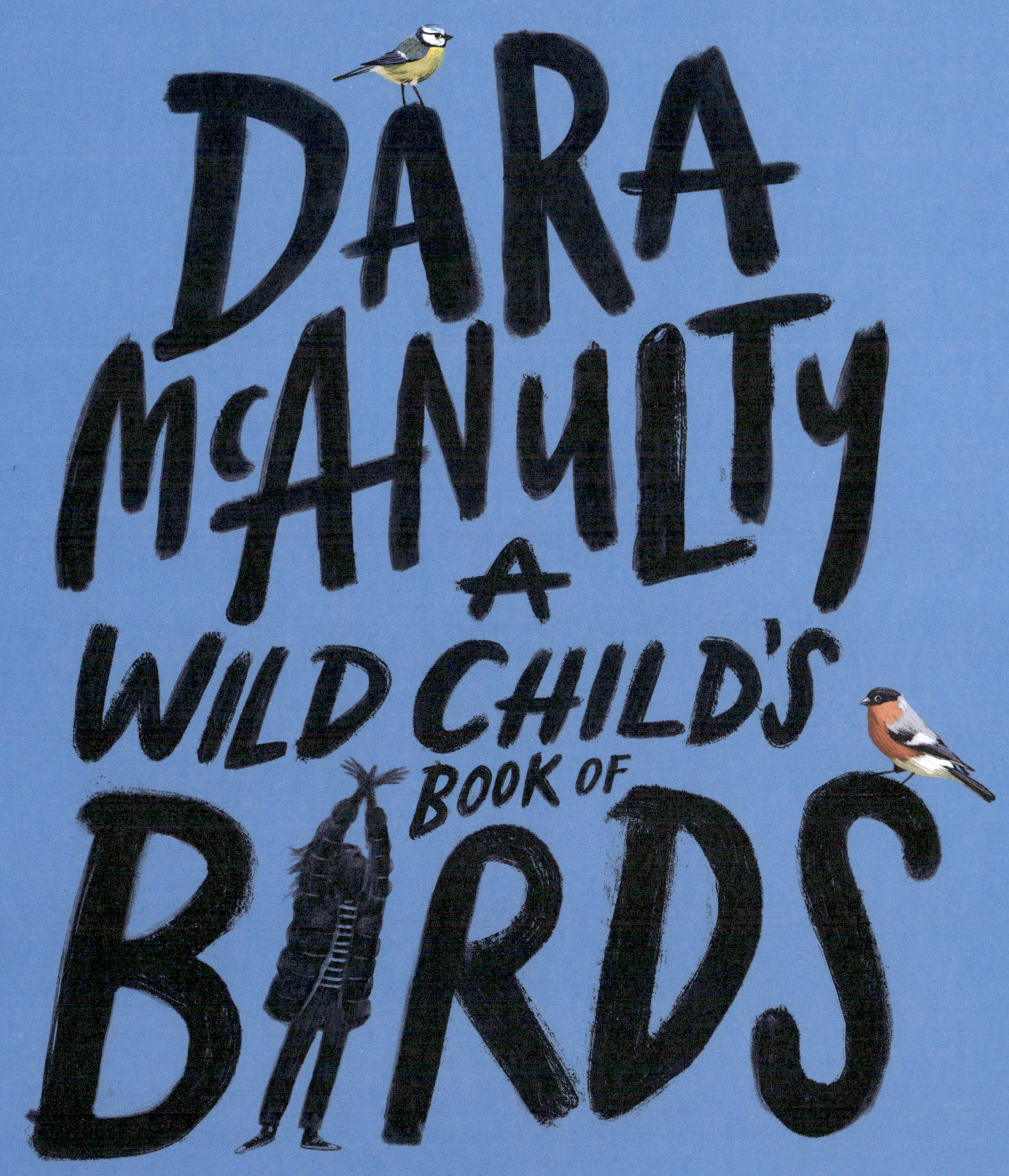

DARA McANULTY
A WILD CHILD'S BOOK OF BIRDS

ILLUSTRATED BY
BARRY FALLS

MACMILLAN CHILDREN'S BOOKS

First published 2022 by Macmillan Children's Books
an imprint of Pan Macmillan
The Smithson, 6 Briset Street, London EC1M 5NR
EU representative: Macmillan Publishers Ireland Ltd, 1st Floor,
The Liffey Trust Centre, 117–126 Sheriff Street Upper, Dublin 1, D01 YC43
Associated companies throughout the world
www.panmacmillan.com

ISBN 978-1-5290-7075-0

Text copyright © Dara McAnulty 2022
Illustrations copyright © Barry Falls 2022

The right of Dara McAnulty and Barry Falls to be identified as the
author and illustrator of this work has been asserted by them in accordance
with the Copyright, Designs and Patents Act 1988.

All rights reserved. No part of this publication may be reproduced,
stored in a retrieval system, or transmitted, in any form or by any means
(electronic, mechanical, photocopying, recording or otherwise),
without the prior written permission of the publisher.

Pan Macmillan does not have any control over, or any responsibility for,
any author or third-party websites referred to in or on this book.

1 3 5 7 9 8 6 4 2

A CIP catalogue record for this book is available from the British Library.

Design: Janene Spencer

Printed and bound in China

This book is sold subject to the condition that it shall not,
by way of trade or otherwise, be lent, resold, hired out,
or otherwise circulated without the publisher's prior consent
in any form of binding or cover other than that in which
it is published and without a similar condition including this
condition being imposed on the subsequent purchaser.

CONTENTS

INTRODUCTION	1
1. SPRING	2
What's Happening in the Bird World in Spring?	6
Why Do Birds Sing?	8
My Top Five Songbirds	9
Nests	10
Birds in Literature	13
Recording Techniques and Birdwatching	14
2. SUMMER	16
What's Going on in the Bird World During Summer?	20
Beaks and Bills	22
My Top Five Birds of Prey	26
3. AUTUMN	28
What Do Birds Do in Autumn?	32
Feathers	34
Types of Feather	36
Moulting	37
The Power of Flight	38
Phenomenal Feet	39
4. WINTER	40
What are Birds up to in Winter?	44
Birds in Urban Areas	46
Captivating Corvids	48
Feed the Birds	50
A Note on Cleaning Bird Feeders	51
LATIN NAMES	52
GLOSSARY	54
HELPFUL ORGANISATIONS	57
ABOUT THE AUTHOR AND ILLUSTRATOR	57

Hello Wild Child

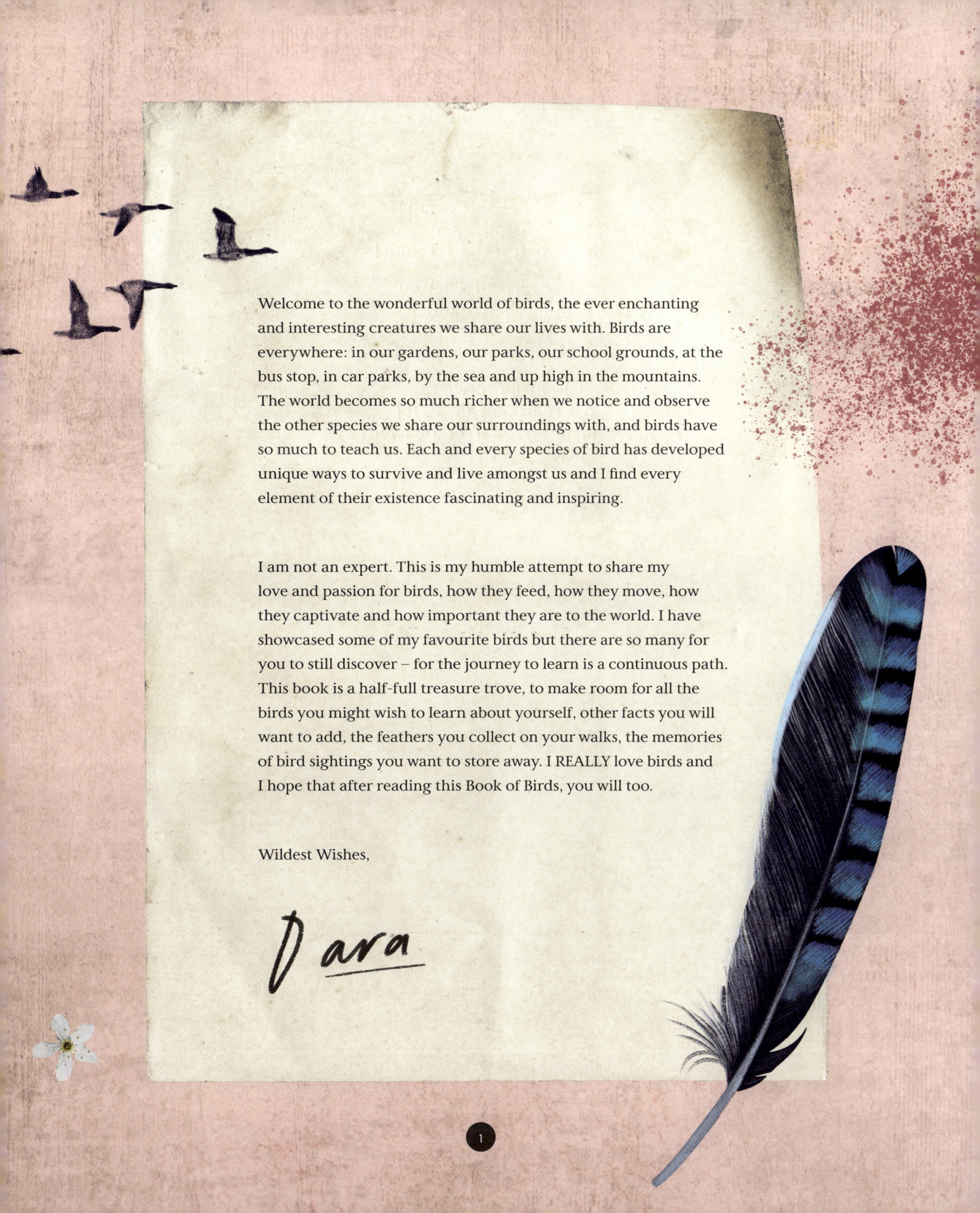

Welcome to the wonderful world of birds, the ever enchanting and interesting creatures we share our lives with. Birds are everywhere: in our gardens, our parks, our school grounds, at the bus stop, in car parks, by the sea and up high in the mountains. The world becomes so much richer when we notice and observe the other species we share our surroundings with, and birds have so much to teach us. Each and every species of bird has developed unique ways to survive and live amongst us and I find every element of their existence fascinating and inspiring.

I am not an expert. This is my humble attempt to share my love and passion for birds, how they feed, how they move, how they captivate and how important they are to the world. I have showcased some of my favourite birds but there are so many for you to still discover – for the journey to learn is a continuous path. This book is a half-full treasure trove, to make room for all the birds you might wish to learn about yourself, other facts you will want to add, the feathers you collect on your walks, the memories of bird sightings you want to store away. I REALLY love birds and I hope that after reading this Book of Birds, you will too.

Wildest Wishes,

Dara

SPRING

At dawn's first light, upon rooftop or tree,
sweetly sings robin and blackbird, farewell to frosty dew.

Other birds join the fanfare. Blue tit, chaffinch, wren and thrush!
A choir fills the airspace, whether in city, farm or woods.

Everywhere there is music, a joyful
building up of song. It's nature's way
of inviting you, to heed its urgent call.

SPRING

As the days become brighter and spring sun warms your cheeks swifts come in parties. To celebrate. It's spring!

Swallows arrive too, with their bubbling squirts and squeaks. Here come the house martins, our sky is now complete.

Deep in the forest, an invisible cuckoo calls. Its resounding two-beat chime ricochets all around.

Is it a chiffchaff or willow warbler? It's very hard to tell, but listen very carefully, is the chiffchaff singing its name?

In spring the birds are dazzling, busily building their nests. Intricate avian cathedrals to nurture and to care. So, what is nature singing? This performance plays for you, connecting all your senses, to see the world anew.

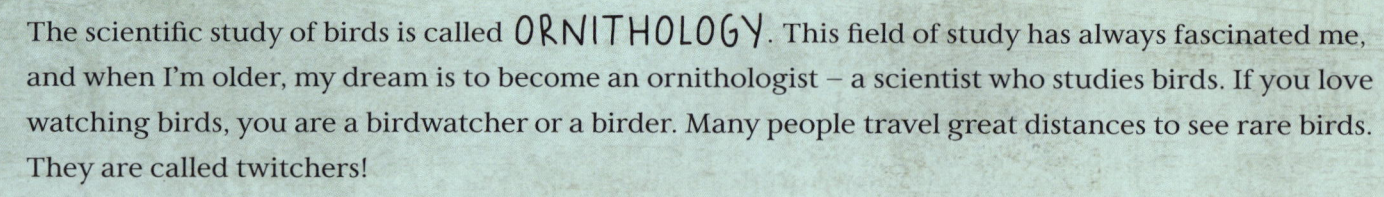

The scientific study of birds is called ORNITHOLOGY. This field of study has always fascinated me, and when I'm older, my dream is to become an ornithologist – a scientist who studies birds. If you love watching birds, you are a birdwatcher or a birder. Many people travel great distances to see rare birds. They are called twitchers!

WHAT'S HAPPENING IN THE BIRD WORLD IN SPRING?

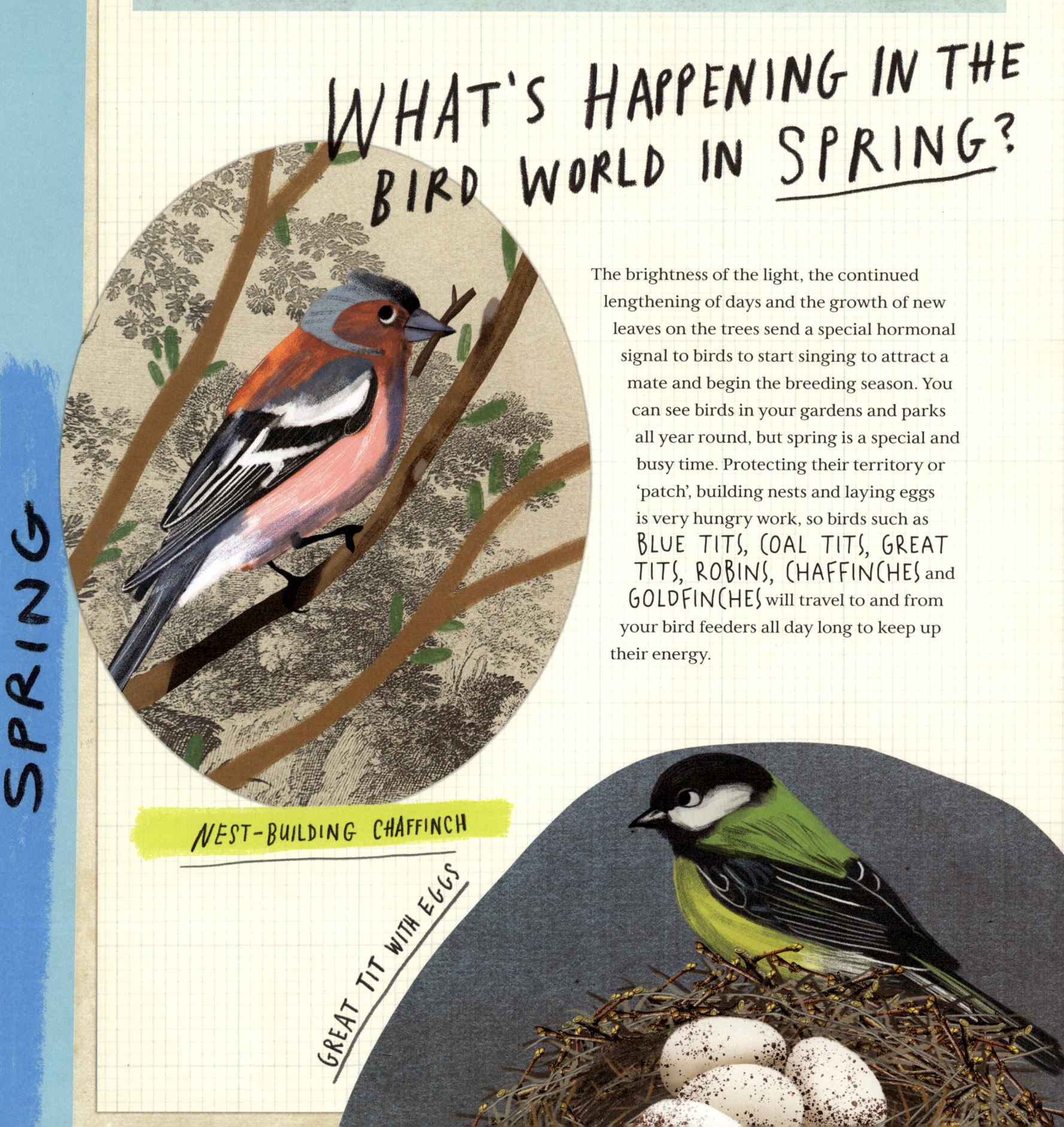

The brightness of the light, the continued lengthening of days and the growth of new leaves on the trees send a special hormonal signal to birds to start singing to attract a mate and begin the breeding season. You can see birds in your gardens and parks all year round, but spring is a special and busy time. Protecting their territory or 'patch', building nests and laying eggs is very hungry work, so birds such as BLUE TITS, COAL TITS, GREAT TITS, ROBINS, CHAFFINCHES and GOLDFINCHES will travel to and from your bird feeders all day long to keep up their energy.

SPRING

NEST-BUILDING CHAFFINCH

GREAT TIT WITH EGGS

The best bird food for your spring bird feeder is black sunflower seeds, sunflower hearts, suet nibbles and mealworms. BLACKBIRDS, THRUSHES and DUNNOCKS like to feed on the ground, so they will really appreciate a small amount of scattered bird seed. Fat balls and peanuts should be avoided at this time of year, as adult birds may feed these to their nestlings and could be harmful. Please don't feed bread to your garden birds, or to the ducks at your local park – it is very low in nutrients, yet it fills up the bird's stomach leaving no room for nutritious seeds and good fats. Birds do love some grated cheese though, a small amount on your bird table is great for spring feeding.

If your local park or nature reserve has a lake, watch male MALLARD DUCKS preen the feathers of the female or observe the courtship dance between GREAT-CRESTED GREBES as they rise up in the water with offerings of pond weed as they elegantly swivel and shake their heads.

GREAT-CRESTED GREBES

Birds need to look their best for the spring season so BLUE TITS eat a lot of green caterpillars, so their breast is beautifully bright yellow. BLACK-HEADED GULLS grow a chocolate-brown feathered hood to attract females – so they are not really black-headed gulls at all!

PREENING MALLARDS

BLACK-HEADED GULL

BLACKCAP

WHY DO BIRDS SING?

Birdsong is one of the most enchanting and interesting facets of the natural world. It fills our days with joy and beauty. The dawn chorus is something naturalists look forward to after a long winter. But there are also some very important reasons why birds sing.

Male birds sing to attract a mate as females are drawn to the best and most robust song. Female birds do sing, but less loudly than males.

Birds sing to defend their territory, it's their way of saying 'This is my patch!'

Most birds only sing in spring and summer during the breeding season. It's always bittersweet when the air has lost its music.

SPRING

NIGHTINGALE

SYRINX

Songbirds have a very cool organ called a SYRINX, which holds their vocal cords, deep down in their chest. They have two sets of vocal cords which allow them to sing two songs at once and in harmony with themselves!

MY TOP FIVE SONGBIRDS

NIGHTINGALES are very rare, and their song is most famed all over the world. They sing at night with the moon and stars. I heard lots of nightingales when I was in Berlin, Germany. I have never forgotten their melodic and exultant music, gushing like a musical waterfall. A loud spectrum of tweets, whistles, pipes and flutes. Flamboyant and yet, also restrained. The poet Tennyson wrote that 'the music of the moon sleeps in the pale eggs of the nightingale'.

BLACKCAPS are musical virtuosos. Their song has many notes and varying tempos. Keep a watch out for them perching on branch tops in summer woodlands. They can mimic other birds though, so bring your binoculars if you have a pair.

ROBINS sing all year round to hold their territories during summer and winter. They may look cute, but they are very aggressive, but yes . . . still cute! To me their song sounds melancholic, which for such a bright and restless bird makes them surprising and interesting.

BLACKBIRDS are known as the Beethoven of birds due to their complex musicality and mellow notes. Watch them sing from chimney pots and television aerials as well as treetops. They are true performers with a wide repertoire of notes.

SKYLARKS are the most joyous of all the songbirds. They rise in the air as if they are pulled by puppet strings and sing whilst they hover in the air, wings beating very fast. Their flight song is elaborate, melodious and truly spectacular. An ascending skylark in song is rarely forgotten. Skylarks can reach heights of three hundred metres before descending like a parachute to the ground before rising once more in sumptuous song.

NESTS

LONG-TAILED TIT

LONG-TAILED TITS have a beautifully constructed nest that is made of moss and, surprisingly, gauzy spider webs. They deftly weave the threads in and around the mossy enclosure to give it some extra strength and resilience. Did you know that spider webs are five times the strength of steel? Wow! It's a very intricate nest and takes three weeks to build. This little bird lines its newly built nesting place with approximately 1,500 feathers to make it snug and warm!

WREN

SPRING

WRENS are incredibly busy birds and make more than one nest, with the males crafting six to twelve nests in any available nook or cranny. The female then chooses which one she likes best and lines it with an offering of feathers. Not all of the nests will go to waste, though, as multiple females may try to occupy the male's many abodes.

The **GUILLEMOT** is a pretty extreme and fascinating bird, living high upon clifftops with only a small ledge to call home. The steep rock face is clustered with many other birds – the name for this is a colony. It's very noisy on a sea-bird cliff! Guillemots lay a single jade and black egg. It is very beautiful and specially shaped, so it doesn't roll away. It's a precarious business nesting on clifftops! Just one hour after it hatches, the little fledgling will make a leap from the cliff using its incredibly fluffy feathers to bounce and roll its way to the ocean below.

GUILLEMOT

BARN OWL

BARN OWLS are an interesting bird. As their name suggests, they usually try to nest, in well, barns! They will find a cosy corner in between the eaves of the roof. They will also nest inside old trees and they love nest boxes. When they choose a nest, they keep it for life, so we need to respect their place of residence. Barn owls are very rare, so it's important they are not disturbed during the nesting season.

A group of eggs laid at the same time is called a CLUTCH.

BROOD is the name given to a clutch of eggs hatched at the same time, by the same parents.

RINGED PLOVERS are ground-nesting birds and nest on the seashore amidst speckled pebbles. The eggs mimic the pattern of the pebbles, which keeps them safe from predators. Excellent camouflage! It's very important when ringed plovers are nesting (there's usually a sign) that you leave them in peace and keep dogs on a lead.

RINGED PLOVER

REED WARBLER

CUCKOO

Did you know that CUCKOOS don't build nests? They are brood parasites, which means they drop their eggs in another bird's nest! Their favourites are meadow pipit, reed warbler and dunnock. Astoundingly, the cuckoo egg looks just like the host egg and so the adult birds cannot tell the difference. When the cuckoo has hatched, it pushes the other eggs out of the nest with its back, so it is the only bird left and there is no competition for food. Then, the adult birds have to raise and feed the cuckoo. These foster parents have no idea that there is an imposter in the nest. The chick is a ferocious feeder! Look at the size difference! Yikes!

WHAT SHOULD YOU DO IF YOU FIND A BIRD'S NEST?

Nesting birds are protected by law and you must never knowingly disturb a nest, always observe at a distance. Disturbing a bird's nest may cause the parents to abandon their chicks. If you regularly visit a nest, you could leave a scent for predators! When you're a little older, you can help monitor nests or become a bird ringer (when birds are given bands to help ornithologists identify and learn from birds and follow their journeys) for the British Trust for Ornithology, which is a wonderful thing for a young naturalist to do!

SPRING

BIRDS IN LITERATURE

Birds have long been revered in culture all around the world. They are seen as emblems of beauty, hope and perseverance. Their flight, wondrous song, plumage and curious behaviours have inspired poets for centuries. Here are a couple of my favourite poems. Do you have a favourite?

from TO A SKYLARK

Hail to thee, blithe Spirit!
　Bird thou never wert,
That from Heaven, or near it,
　Pourest thy full heart
In profuse strains of unpremeditated art.

Higher still and higher
　From the earth thou springest
Like a cloud of fire;
　The blue deep thou wingest,
And singing still dost soar, and soaring ever singest.

In the golden lightning
　Of the sunken sun,
O'er which clouds are bright'ning,
　Thou dost float and run;
Like an unbodied joy whose race is just begun.

PERCY SHELLEY

EMILY DICKINSON

"Hope" is the thing with feathers –
That perches in the soul –
And sings the tune without the words –
And never stops – at all –

And sweetest – in the Gale – is heard –
And sore must be the storm –
That could abash the little Bird
That kept so many warm –

I've heard it in the chillest land –
And on the strangest Sea –
Yet, never, in Extremity,
It asked a crumb – of Me.

RECORDING TECHNIQUES AND BIRDWATCHING

Recording birds in your garden or when out on your walk is a very enriching experience. When you observe and record birds over a period of time, you begin to notice interesting patterns and can learn a lot about bird behaviour. You could record which food certain birds like best – do they feed more in sun than in rain? There are so many intriguing facets to the life of a bird, and you can be a part of their story too!

SPRING

TOOLS OF THE TRADE

NOTEBOOK AND PENCIL – record the date and weather. Make a list of the birds you see and make a tally if there are more than one of each species.

SKETCH PAD AND PENCILS/PAINTS – it's wonderful to draw the birds you see. It doesn't have to be perfect! Try it and see!

MOBILE PHONE – to record birdsong and film your birds. Capture the daily behaviours of your local avian population to see and hear subtle changes. There are also apps which can help you identify birds and their song. My favourite identification app is the 'Collins Birdguide' – it has everything a young birder might need.

CAMERA – photographing birds can become a life-long passion. Start off with a simple camera. As you grow older and your interest deepens, you can broaden your equipment. Check second-hand websites and stores as photography can be expensive.

BINOCULARS – to see the bird world through. Especially good for searching amongst foliage and finding birds which are far away.

If you're outside, dress very warmly and stretch out your muscles every so often. Waiting on birds requires patience but is very rewarding when the bird you've been waiting for shows up!

You can visit special bird hides at nature reserves to comfortably observe birds. These are fantastic for spotting birds you wouldn't find in your garden!

DATABASES TO RECORD YOUR SIGHTINGS AND CITIZEN SCIENCE PROJECTS TO GET INVOLVED IN

iNATURALIST is a great online space for recording all wildlife, including your birds.

The BTO BIRDTRACK mobile phone app lets you record bird sightings all over the world, and, once again, helps scientists monitor sightings and populations.

BTO GARDEN BIRDWATCH is a great year-round citizen science project. Recording birds for this survey really helps ornithologists who are protecting and conserving garden bird populations and provides very interesting data for them to use!

RSPB BIG GARDEN BIRDWATCH happens in January every year. It's an hour-long bird-spotting survey and great fun. Brilliant for all the family, it also has a school's pack to get your teachers and friends involved. Another great citizen science opportunity to help protect and monitor garden birds.

SUM

MER

The trees are in full leaf, fully dressed, with burgeoning branches. Birdsong now accompanies the buzzing hum of flowering meadows.

Every corner is bursting with life, so full of magic. Birds are flying back and forth to feed their hungry fledglings.

The air is full of energy, a wondrous rhapsody of action. It's nature's way of inviting you down a path of fascination.

As the days become hotter, in early morning light, nests are quietly abandoned, as new wings flutter to flight.

SUMMER

Nervous parents hover, still feeding hungry mouths,
for the little ones aren't quite ready to venture far from boughs.

Under the eaves of rooftops, in crevices and cracks,
swallows and swifts build later, their nests now finally intact.

*As summer draws to closing, the skies will gradually clear
of all the brightening busyness, no birdsong now to hear.*

*Know that life is circling though, as nature is ever turning,
there are many delights forthcoming, to fulfil your wildest yearnings.*

WHAT'S GOING ON IN THE BIRD WORLD DURING SUMMER?

SUMMER

As the temperature rises and the days grow to their longest, birds are hyperactively busy. Chicks are FLEDGING the nests, but parents must be on their guard to keep their little ones close and protect them from predators. If you have a garden bird population and have been feeding them, it is such an exciting moment to see FLEDGLINGS emerge from the nest and into your garden. You can hear the GARRULOUS chattering of baby birds begging for food as the adults continue to care for their young outside the nest. To know you are helping future populations is a wonderful thing.

FLEDGLING HOUSE SPARROW

When the young fledge the nest, they do not return. They have outgrown the nest and will spend the night together, roosting in trees out of sight. It's a very nerve-wracking time! The young birds already possess fantastic instincts and survival skills such as how to camouflage, find food, work as a group, recognise predators and attract mates successfully, but they still need the support of their parents just like you do.

ROBIN — FLEDGLING — ADULT

Most baby birds look like a bedraggled version of their parents. But robins look very different. Their chest is speckly brown at first, as their beautiful red breast needs extra time to develop. Without their bright colouring, they can camouflage too.

Swifts are such incredible birds. After a short period of exercising their wings by doing press-ups (yes!) and peering out from the nest entrance, they fly from nest to sky and immediately begin their long migration journey to Africa with the other fledglings. Swifts do everything 'on the wing' — they eat and sleep whilst flying! I just find this so very remarkable.

SWIFT

If you haven't got a garden, pay your local park a visit. Watch parent MALLARDS and their line of ducklings sail in lakes, adult swans with their cygnets, alongside other species such as COOTS, MOORHENS, TEALS and POCHARDS. Ever looked at the feet of a MOORHEN? They are very strange and look like dinosaur feet! Did you know that for a whole entire month, ducks cannot fly? During this period, they must lose and replace their flight feathers and drake (male) birds look like females as they lose their brightest feathers first to give protection against predators. This process is called MOULTING.

Adult birds look very scraggly during summer. They have been working tremendously hard, feeding and looking after their chicks. They must fly to and from the nest many times each day, not just to feed, but to remove the 'faecal sac' or bird poo far away to keep the nest clean, and safe from predators.

MOORHEN

During the last weeks of summer, your garden birds will visit less frequently as they go off to forage on wild fruits and berries such as blackberries. The skies become quieter as birds no longer need to sing, but don't worry, there are lots of amazing happenings in autumn.

COMMON TEAL

BEAKS and BILLS

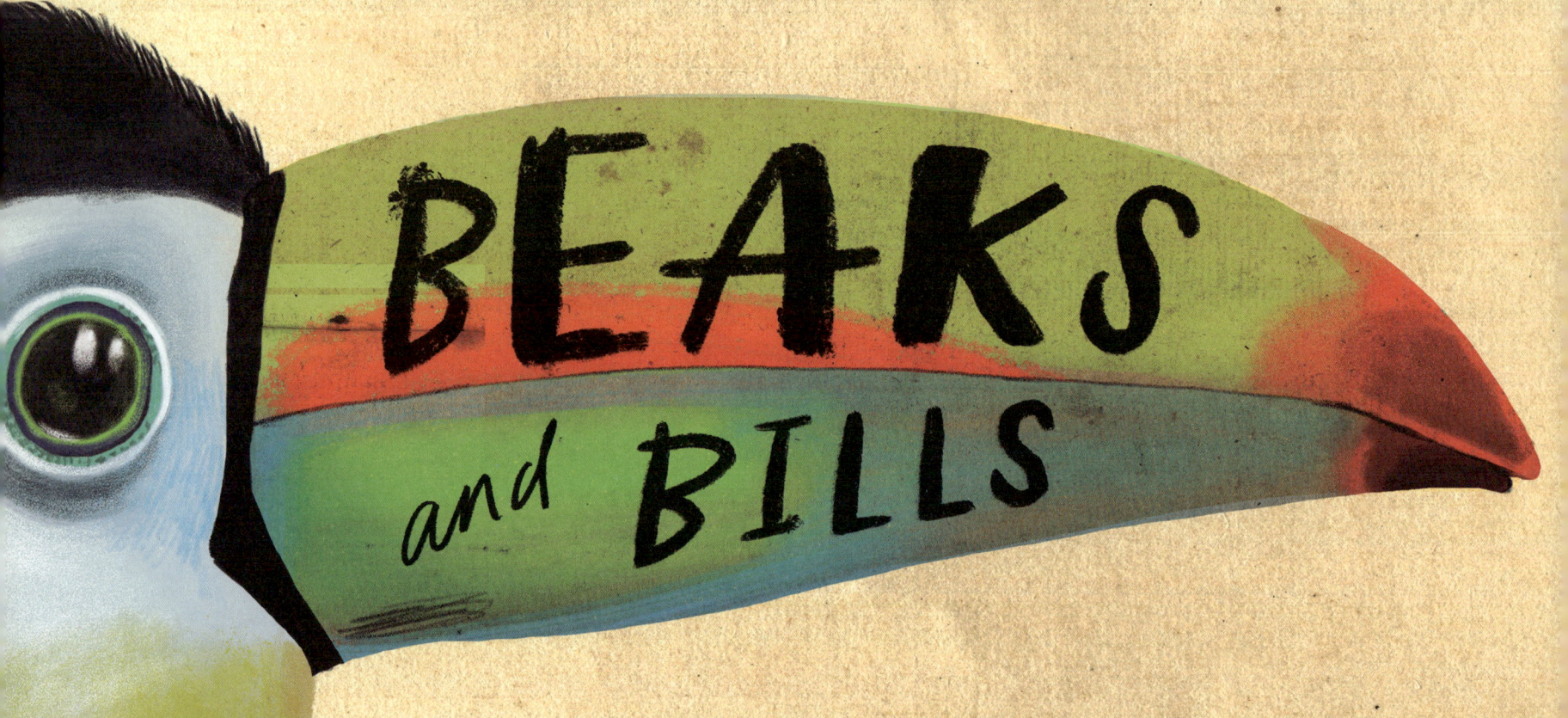

SUMMER

Beaks, or bills, are the toothless mouth of a bird. Beaks are composed of a bony core covered in a layer of tough keratin (which is what your nails are made of). The upper half is called the MAXILLA and the lower half is called the MANDIBLE. Birds also have tongues made from bone and cartilage.

WHY DO BIRDS HAVE DIFFERENT BEAKS?

The most basic and vital function of any living creature is how it gets its food and many species develop special physical adaptations to best suit their environment, so they can survive... This observation led to one of the most incredible scientific discoveries, forever changing our understanding of how life evolved.

It all started with the famous naturalist, Charles Darwin, visiting the Galápagos Islands in 1835. He collected different types of finch and observed that, although they looked similar, birds from different islands had different beaks. Darwin realised that the shape of the birds' beaks allowed them to survive on the food that was available on their islands; birds with long, pointed beaks, for example, could pick seeds out of cactus fruits, or pluck insects off the ground, while short, strong beaks were better suited to a diet of nuts. In total, fourteen species of finch had evolved from just one ancestor – each adapted to its unique habitat and diet.

Our native finches such as SISKIN, GOLDFINCH, BULLFINCH, TWITE, REDPOLL, BRAMBLING, GREENFINCH and CHAFFINCH all have a varied diet but are primarily seed-eating birds with similar bills. The HAWFINCH has a larger, more powerful bill which it uses to crush cherry and plum stones. CROSSBILLS' unusual beak is an adaptation which allows them to extract seeds from conifer trees.

NORTH AMERICA · EUROPE · ATLANTIC OCEAN · AFRICA · SOUTH AMERICA

GALÁPAGOS ISLANDS

CHARLES DARWIN

DARWIN'S FINCHES
MANGROVE FINCH
MEDIUM TREE FINCH
LARGE TREE FINCH
LARGE GROUND FINCH
TOOL-USING FINCH
SMALL TREE FINCH
MEDIUM GROUND FINCH
SMALL GROUND FINCH
INSECT EATERS
VEGETARIAN TREE FINCH
BERRY EATER
COCOS ISLAND FINCH
SHARP-BEAKED GROUND FINCH
LARGE CACTUS FINCH
WARBLER FINCH
SEED EATERS
CACTUS EATERS
CACTUS FINCH
FINCH ADAPTATIONS
INSECT EATERS
ANCESTRAL FINCH

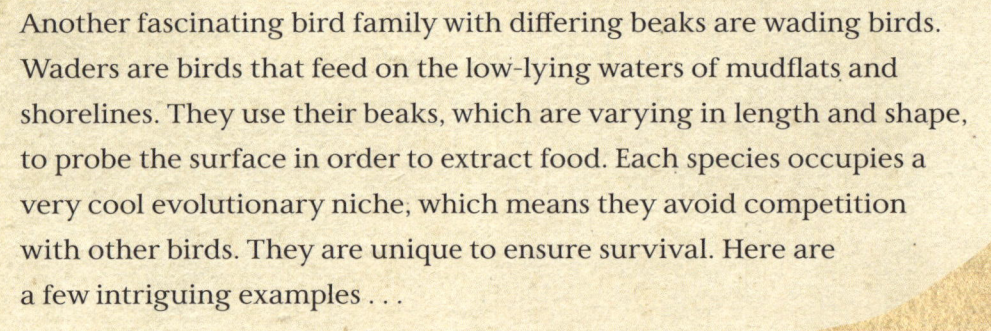

Another fascinating bird family with differing beaks are wading birds. Waders are birds that feed on the low-lying waters of mudflats and shorelines. They use their beaks, which are varying in length and shape, to probe the surface in order to extract food. Each species occupies a very cool evolutionary niche, which means they avoid competition with other birds. They are unique to ensure survival. Here are a few intriguing examples . . .

CURLEWS use their long-curved beaks to catch ragworms deep within the sand. The shape of their bill allows them to remove the worms from the ground without breaking them so they don't lose any of the precious food.

TURNSTONES use their small wedge-shaped bills to flip over rocks, hence the name, to reveal insects, crustaceans and molluscs. They even scavenge around seaweed and eat carrion (dead animals)!

AVOCETS have an upturned, elegant bill. Long and slender, they use it like a delicate shovel, as they swish and swipe the water, sweeping up food. They love shrimp and sandhoppers.

SUMMER

CURLEW

TURNSTONE

AVOCET

WOODPECKER

WOODPECKERS' powerfully sharp beaks are like drills, which they use to chip into tree bark to find insects. Their bristly tongue is covered in a sticky substance, allowing them to easily extract insects from their drilling holes.

HERONS have long, sharply pointed beaks which can stab fish under the water. See them stalking the rivers and coasts prowling for food.

SNIPES have a very cool hinged upper beak tip which is full of tingling nerves, helping them to locate worms under the mud and gobble them up whole.

All birds of prey have dagger-like beaks, allowing them to rip apart meat and eat their food.

SNIPE

HERON

MY TOP 5 BIRDS OF PREY

Birds of prey hunt other animals for food. The word 'raptor' comes from the Latin word 'rapere', which means to seize or plunder. They are some of our most spectacular birds, with their soaring wings, stunning plumage and strong talons. Here are five of my favourites!

Found in upland moors and heathland, HEN HARRIERS are diurnal hunters. They use their amazing sense of hearing to locate their prey, which is mainly birds such as meadow pipits and small mammals. Hen harriers are extremely rare and, sadly, their numbers are falling rapidly due to persecution, habitat and biodiversity loss. The Royal Society for the Protection of Birds (RSPB) has done wonderful work to help preserve the hen harrier, such as nest monitoring, satellite tagging, public awareness campaigns and habitat restoration. Hen harriers hold a very special place in my heart because I have had the great privilege of watching their magnificent sky dancing, a circling courtship flight dance between the male and the female. I also campaign for their safety: birds sometimes need us to sing for them and help to conserve them for future generations.

Brought back from the brink of extinction from a surviving Welsh population to other areas of the UK and Ireland, the RED KITE reintroduction project is one of the most successful bird conservation efforts by the RSPB! Red kites are scavengers, which means they eat dead animals! These resplendent raptors are very special to me as when I was fourteen years old, I raised some money by doing a long hike in winter, so I could help fund satellite tags for red kites in Northern Ireland. These satellite tags helped ecologists learn about their behaviour and to help science and conservation.

The fastest sky hunter on the planet, the PEREGRINE FALCON, rises high in the sky and stoops, with wings tucked in tight, to catch its prey, mostly pigeons, in mid-flight. As it dive-bombs it reaches speeds of up to 320 kmh.
It travels with such speed it has to close off its nostrils to reduce air pressure so that it can breathe. This prevents lung damage and enables its unparalleled pace. Peregrines can also spot their target from up to three kilometres away with binocular vision. Locking their prey in sight, they swiftly catch them in their bright yellow claws. What a spectacle! What a bird!

The greatest field hunter of all, with the sharpest of eyes that can even see ultraviolet light! This superpower helps them see the urine trails of mice and voles as they scurry through the undergrowth. KESTRELS can hover almost like magic: head and body completely still whilst the wind ruffles their feathers, they carefully target their prey, and like a stone they drop and snatch it with blinding accuracy. They can even spot a tiny beetle from fifty metres away! Their main prey are voles and other rodents. An old country name for the kestrel is windhover. If you watch how they hunt, effortlessly flickering their wings whilst suspended in the air, you'll see why.

Did you know owls are birds of prey too? I will never forget the moment I held a female BARN OWL in my hands. I was working with ornithologists to help monitor their weight after the breeding season. Such a stunningly majestic bird. They are mainly crepuscular, meaning they also like to hunt during dawn and dusk, but they are also nocturnal as they are very active at night. They sail through the night like ghosts. Have you ever heard their eerie screeching? Their feathers are super light, which means they can glide silently through the air, their bright whiteness startling their prey and making them easy to catch.

Autumn

Light glows soft and golden, leaves swirl to the ground,
wind rushes faster, now swallows and swifts are Africa bound.

The atmosphere is changing as the temperature begins to fall.
Earthy smells as fungi swells, our land will soon be home for
many birds in search of food. Say hello to our autumn friends!

They have travelled in peril to reach us, how very lucky are we
to have these splendid visitors sharing space with you and me.

The skies begin to echo, with trumpets and bugling honking.
Jubilant salutations, a revelling avian carnival.

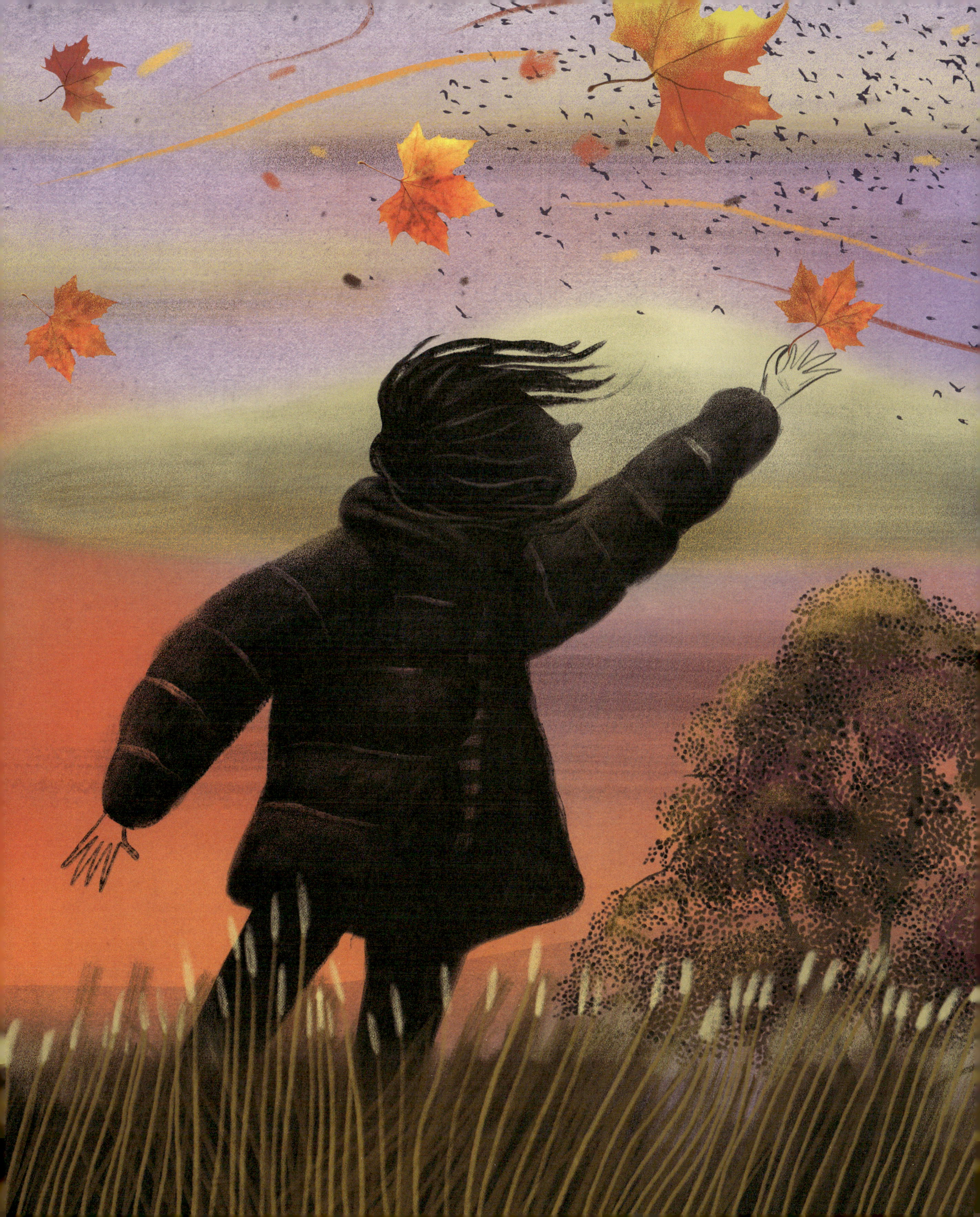

AUTUMN

Brent geese fly in wavy lines, swans in pure white skeins. Gracefully travelling southwards, from the highest clouds to shore and field.

Fallen apples are gobbled, by blackbird, fieldfare and redwing, reaping the autumn harvest, abundant berries of ivy and rowan.

*As the first frosts start to glisten and the trees become gnarly limbs,
your eyes will pinpoint movements, which were previously unseen.*

*Sharpen all your senses, the air is clear as a bell,
all the better to notice robin redbreast's song begin to swell.*

AUTUMN

WHAT DO BIRDS DO IN AUTUMN?

Autumn is a time of wild foraging for birds. It's also accentuated by leaving and returning as a two-way migration begins! Whilst the SWIFTS left our skies in summer, SWALLOWS and HOUSE MARTINS wait until autumn. They come together in large groups to ferociously feed in restless swoops before their journey back to Africa. The gap they leave is quickly filled with many bird species arriving on our coastal shores, mudflats, estuaries and fields. Large numbers of GEESE and SWANS make their way from the far northern countries of Russia, Greenland, Iceland, Canada and Eastern Europe. Many of the birds who arrive in autumn like to spend the entire winter in the UK and Ireland. Watch out for WHITE-FRONTED, PINK FOOTED, BARNACLE and LIGHT-BELLIED BRENT GEESE, WHOOPER and BEWICK'S SWANS.

HOUSE MARTIN

WHITE-FRONTED

LIGHT-BELLIED BRENT

PINK FOOTED

GEESE

The best place to really appreciate these fabulous birds is at a wetland nature reserve. Watch out for WHOOPER SWANS in agricultural fields, feeding on left-over crops, grain and grass. Some migratory birds use our wetlands as their stop-off point in their incredible migratory journeys.

KNOT

14,000 KILOMETRE-JOURNEY

KNOTS begin their 14,000 kilometre-journey after breeding in the Arctic and end it in South America and South Africa! They have a well-earned break in their lengthy mission, by stopping off in our wetlands for a time in winter. Aren't migratory birds just bamboozling? Although it's not fully understood how birds can find their way, particularly in their solo first flight, many scientists have researched some possibilities. Maybe they can detect changes in the strength of the earth's invisible magnetic field? Perhaps using the sun and stars as a compass? It's also possible they use their olfactory system – that's their sense of smell – to detect changes in their environment? Migration is mysterious, utterly confounding, but completely magnificent.

Meanwhile, closer to home, our garden birds will become less frequent as they go in search of nature's larder to feast on berries, nuts, fallen fruits and seeds. If you're lucky to have a wild food source in your garden, you don't need to supplement with bird feeders at this time. It's very important for birds to forage.

THRUSHES, such as REDWING and FIELDFARE migrate to our fields and gardens during the autumn months to escape the harsher winters of northern Europe. They are beautiful birds which are part of the same family as our resident SONG/ MISTLE THRUSHES and BLACKBIRDS. They love to feed on fallen apples.

REDWING THRUSH

AUTUMN

BIRD FEATHERS AND THE POWER OF FLIGHT

Bird feathers are one of the most fascinating and complex parts of nature. Light and delicate in their construction, they provide birds with the ability to fly thousands of feet and hold them high in the air.

WHAT ARE THEY MADE OF?

Ever hear people say that things are as light as a feather? Despite the incredible nature of bird feathers, they are very light, and made from a substance called KERATIN – the very same material that is in reptile scales and claws. In fact, the very first birds evolved from reptiles. The birds which grace our skies today are a wondrous reminder of a very distant past.

Evolution of BIRDS & FEATHERS

Did you know that birds are descended from a group of dinosaurs called PARAVES, which belonged to the THEROPOD FAMILY? Long before dinosaurs became extinct 66 million years ago, this interesting group evolved to develop bird-like features such as feathers, to provide insulation, enable faster movement and give better balance whilst running from predators, just like an ostrich! The most famous link between dinosaur and bird is the ARCHAEOPTERYX which had feathers and wings like a bird and reptilian tail bones and teeth. What we know about the evolution of birds and dinosaurs is constantly changing, illuminated by new fossils unearthed by palaeontologists: scientists who study ancient life. So, the next time you look out your window, you might see birds in a new light!

FEATHERS

ARCHAEOPTERYX MAY HAVE LOOKED LIKE THIS

MODERN-DAY CORMORANT

Feathers give birds the power of flight. They are the only living creature to have them, but they also have other important uses. Feathers are used for fancy displays during the mating season, ruffs having the most ostentatious plumage. Feathers are also used for camouflage. I never see a snipe or woodcock until I accidentally disturb them whilst walking in upland fields and bogs. They are expert hide-and-seekers! The layers of feathers which make up a bird's plumage insulate them, keeping them toasty in cold weather and cooler in the warmer months. Isn't nature amazing?!

Types of Feather

CONTOUR – arranged like roof tiles to cover a bird's body, these feathers are waterproof and give a bird a smooth, sleek outline. Contour feathers are often colourful, with a fluffy, soft part next to the body.

FILOPLUME – mixed among the contours, these wispy feathers act like mammal whiskers. Many scientists think that filoplumes act like little sensors which can detect lost or damaged feathers and replace them. Amazing!

BRISTLE – these feathers are most commonly found on the head and may protect the bird's eyes and face. They help woodpeckers filter the dust that flies out when they drill holes in trees, and they also help owls sense nearby objects. Feathers are super cool!

FLIGHT (WING) – flight feathers are a large type of feather located in the wings and tails. Asymmetric in structure, they are strong, stiff, windproof and essential to flight.

TAIL – arranged in a fan shape, they act as brakes and a steering wheel in flight. Birds usually have six pairs of tail feathers. Other birds use their tail feathers to show off, and these are useless for flight.

SEMIPLUME – these are the soft, fuzzy hidden feathers, which help insulate and regulate body temperature.

DOWN – very similar to semiplume, these feathers are looser and even fluffier. They trap body heat, a little bit like the base layer you might use for sports or hiking.

Moulting

OLD FEATHER
NEW FEATHER

STARLING BEFORE MOULTING

FRESHLY MOULTED STARLING

Feathers work really hard and so have to be replaced, usually at least once every year. Moulting is the process of producing new feathers, which push the old ones out and grow from a follicle, just like our hair. Birds typically moult after breeding and before migration. Notice how scraggly a blue tit looks in August and watch the incredible transformation take place over the course of a few weeks. When a starling moults its feathers, the tips are white, which give them that gorgeous speckled plumage during autumn and winter.

The brave women who campaigned to save birds from the murderous millinery trade!

In July 1921, Emily Williamson, Etta Lemon, Eliza Phillips and Winifred Cavendish-Bentinck, Duchess of Portland, brought change to the bird world and made history by instigating The Importation of Plumage (Prohibition) Act. Feathers in fashion were very popular in Victorian and Edwardian times and resulted in the death of countless birds, the appetite for feathers in hats almost driving birds such as little egrets and great crested grebes to extinction. Emily and her fellow campaigners successfully campaigned for a ban on the import of plumage, and founded the incredible charity which became known as the Royal Society for the Protection of Birds! Their efforts were mainly forgotten until recently, and in November 2021, Eve Shepherd won a public vote to create and erect a celebratory statue of Emily to honour her achievements.

Emily Williamson

The POWER OF FLIGHT

KESTREL

PASSIVE SOARING

ALBATROSS

ACTIVE SOARING

ELLIPTICAL

CROW

HIGH-SPEED WINGS

FALCON

HOVERING

HUMMINGBIRD

Like all things in nature, bird wings are adapted for survival, allowing birds to live and thrive in different environments. There are four main types which give birds special skills.

TYPES OF WING

PASSIVE SOARING wings have long primary feathers which spread out like your fingers, allowing birds to catch rising columns of hot air called thermals and rise higher in the sky. The kestrel, hen harrier, buzzard and all types of eagle have magnificent passive soaring wings.

ACTIVE SOARING wings are long, sleek and narrow. Birds with this type of wing can fly for long distances without flapping their wings. Very dependent on wind currents, gulls and gannets glide through the air, seemingly effortlessly, and can withstand very harsh winds.

ELLIPTICAL WINGS are used for very short bursts of high-speed flight, for taking off from branch or ground and also for manoeuvring through tight spaces. Our garden birds have elliptical wings, as do ravens and other corvids.

HIGH-SPEED WINGS are long and thin like active soaring wings, but are much shorter and allow swifts, ducks, falcons and tern to fly through the air maintaining top speed. These are the turbo wings of the bird world, for the wild racers and long-distance travellers.

HOVERING WINGS are ferociously fast, moving so quickly that the special birds who have them appear to float in the air. As well as having hovering wings, hummingbirds have nerves and muscles for super-fast movement. Hummingbirds only live in the Americas, but we have a cool species of moth called the hummingbird hawkmoth, whose wings move in a similar way.

PHENOMENAL FEET

Birds' legs and feet are diverse, deadly and dramatic. They are specially adapted for different environments, functions and purposes. Some feet work like oars, others grip and catch prey, and some birds don't even have functioning feet! Most birds need very strong and capable feet to balance their weight on two legs. Did you know that the joint we see on birds' legs which bends backwards is actually their ankle? We cannot see most of the bird's legs as they are obscured by fluffy feathers. The foot bone connected to the ankle is called the tarsometatarsus, and the toes, or digits, are fused to the bottom. So birds actually walk on their toes! Woodpeckers have very cool toes. Most birds have four toes (three at the front and one hind toe) but woodpeckers have two toes to the front and two at the back, which gives them the special variation they need to attach to tree trunks. Swifts have evolved to have very short legs as they never land on the ground, but they have powerful feet to hold on to cliffs and walls.

PADDLES

Ducks and swimming birds look so graceful on the water, don't they? Under the surface their webbed feet are working really hard, pushing through the water to propel forwards. They have flexible skin between their toes which helps them paddle along.

GRIPS

The feet of birds of prey are ferociously powerful and are called talons. They have a deadly grip which crushes the smaller birds or mammals these impressive birds need to survive and are strong enough to hold the prey intact during flight. Owls and other raptors look as if they have no legs whilst perching on a tree but watch them extend as they catch their dinner!

STILTS

Waders have really long legs so they can walk, or wade, in deep water. This adaptation means that their feathers stay nice and dry, ready for flight. You will often see wading birds balancing on one leg. This is because birds lose a lot of heat through their legs, and this is how they keep warm.

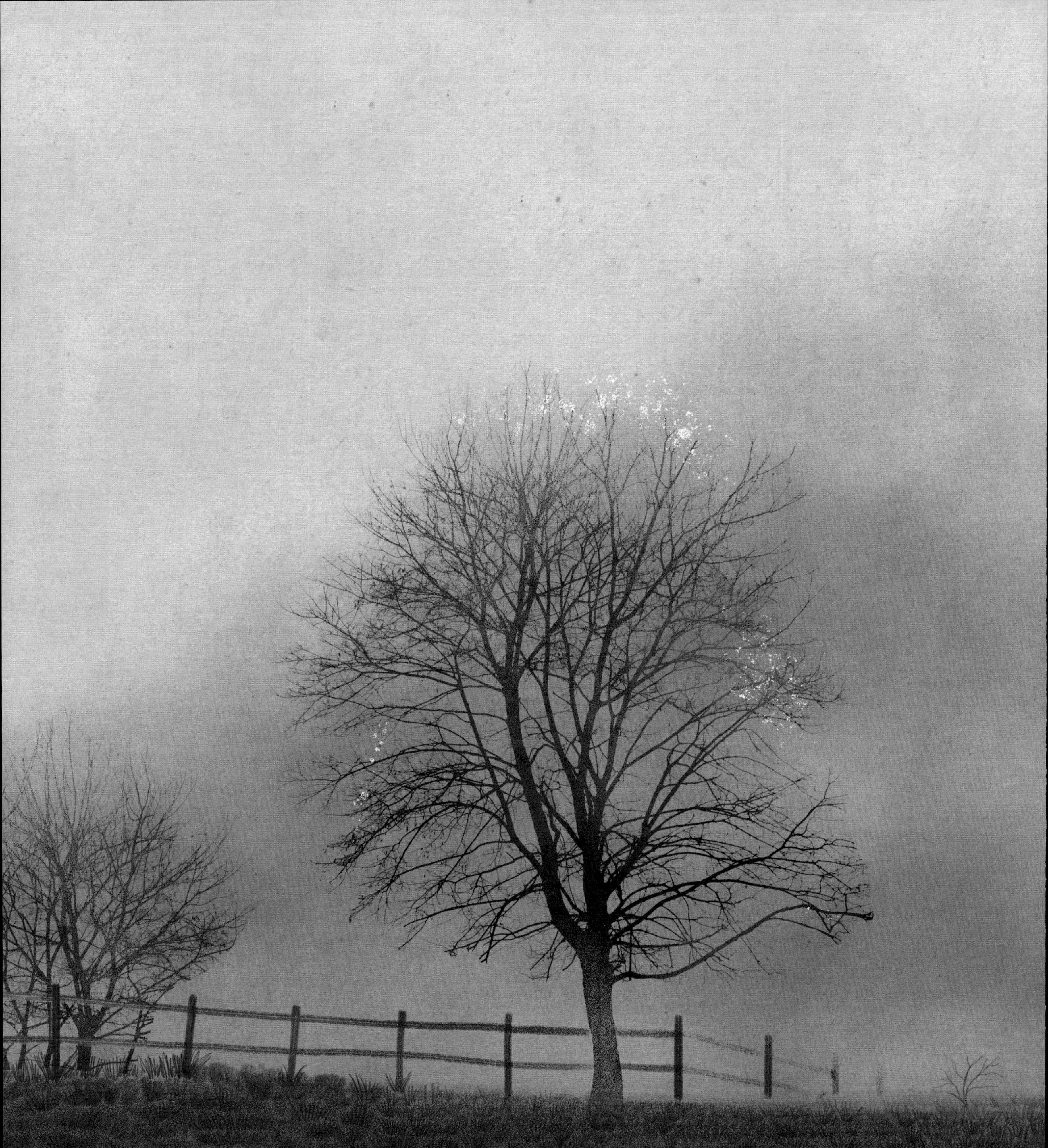

Winter

As darkness engulfs the landscape, for many more hours of each day,
it can seem cold and lifeless outside, but nature has special secrets to share.

Trees are shadow maps of wonder where tribes of sparrows convene.
The birds need you now more than ever, as autumn abundance is but a memory.

Winter snaps and birds come together, to huddle and snuggle up tight,
a line of feathered mumruffins, a wreath of tidley-topes.

In evening light assembling, coming from near and far,
to join the roosting spectacle, whooshing wings, beating fast.

WINTER

Starlings become wind and movement, as countless become one, a pulsing cloud of darkening, rushing out of the sun.

Mistle thrush song resounds, from the bare top branch of a tree, the storm cock begins its nesting before the light of spring.

*Now notice crimson buds of hazel, catkins of the willow.
The circle of life repeating, as circles always do.*

*Winter has its frozen beauty, but wings will crave the light,
early morning will, once again, pour the music out.*

WHAT ARE BIRDS UP TO IN WINTER?

WINTER

As temperatures begin to fall and preparations for the holiday season are well underway, birds are beginning to gather together for safety and warmth. Birds such as LONG-TAILED TITS and WRENS huddle together in quite large groups. Gregarious flocks of garden birds such as SPARROWS, BLUE/GREAT/COAL TITS and GOLDFINCHES gather together in a chattering cacophony. Safety in numbers is key during winter to successfully forage and keep predators at bay when they are vulnerable to cold and scarcity of food. Keep your ears pricked for the wonderful bird sounds echoing from bare branches of shrubs and trees.

Winter is by far the most arduous time for our feathered friends and it's the season when they need our help most. So, fill up your garden bird table and watch the birds gobble and bicker over food. You will be a real hero of the bird world as birds are most likely to die of starvation and cold when the weather harshly howls. It is also a lovely idea to put up roosting boxes in your garden for wrens and robins, a place to shelter from the elements. During winter, wrens roosted together in the empty swallow nest in our little woodshed. We saw six little heads peering over the top! If you had swallows nesting, please leave their nests up so that other birds can shelter from the chilly wind.

WRENS IN A ROOSTING BOX

ROBIN REDBREAST

The ROBIN is synonymous with Christmas, adorning cards everywhere, but far from being the sweet bird in the snow, robins are at their most aggressive in winter, when they fight off invaders to keep their territory for the incoming breeding season.

STARLING MURMURATION

Winter weather may be relentless, but it is also the time of miraculous happenings. MURMURATION, a delightful word, is the term used to describe a monumental flock of birds, dancing together in the sky. STARLINGS are synonymous with murmurations, but KNOTS, a coastal bird, also display this behaviour. If you're lucky enough to see a murmuration, you might also see a peregrine falcon penetrating the cloud of birds, looking for easy prey. It's such an astonishing sight to see.

During the last throes of winter, many birds begin courting and nesting. RAPTORS are very active in February, and you might see pairs tumble and twirl in the sky whilst calling to each other. MISTLE THRUSHES, HERONS and CROWS also start building nests in February. However, many garden birds are also beginning to nest earlier and earlier, which is an indicator that climate change is affecting breeding and nesting behaviour. The impact of this is being studied by ornithologists and is an important area of research.

NEST-BUILDING MISTLE THRUSH

BIRDS IN URBAN AREAS

Since the Industrial Revolution, which began in the mid-1700s, humans have moved from the countryside to find work in cities. As our population grows, we take up more and more space in the landscape, and it has become very important to live peacefully with nature and the birds that live alongside us, especially as many species are declining. Birds such as starlings, pigeons, crows and gulls are considered pests in urban areas, but they are also encouraged by our littering and the way we dispose of food – media sensationalism doesn't help their reputation either! They are highly adaptable and intelligent species and can exploit new food sources with fervour. Starlings and some gulls, however, are on the 'Red List' of birds which are rapidly declining. Human actions are changing the way birds have traditionally lived and they are adapting to the way we are shaping the world. Sometimes this can have a positive effect, but it is also hard to see what the future will hold for our city birds.

Here are a few interesting city birds:

WAXWING – one day, I was about to get in the car at our local garden centre when I heard some very loud chattering that was unfamiliar. I sought it out, and there, in the trees, was a flock of garrulous waxwings. I soon learnt that this can be a common occurrence in cities and towns, especially if there are any rowan or cotoneaster berries to be had. Waxwings will visit us during winter when the berries are scarce in northern Europe.

RING-NECKED PARAKEETS – these vibrant, energetic birds are not a native species. When I first visited London, they took me completely by surprise: an exotic flash of colour, especially on a dull winter's day. Originally from Africa and India, they began to populate the capital when they either escaped from captivity or were deliberately released. It's a mystery!

WINTER

WAXWING

PARAKEET

SWIFTS – I will never forget the screaming summer swifts of my childhood, growing up in inner-city Belfast. Historically, swifts nested in trees and cliffs, but due to lack of habitat and urbanisation, swifts now rely on older buildings. Cities, such as Belfast and Oxford, are providing havens for swifts in the form of nest boxes. This community effort could save swifts from declining as their numbers are shrinking with each passing year.

Honorary mentions go to the PIGEON and the PEREGRINE FALCON, the prey and the predator frequenting many city skies. Peregrines love to live and nest in city cathedrals. Like living gargoyles, they perch and watch the world go by. Pigeons or ROCK DOVES, their prey, really are beautiful birds, I think. They have an iridescent green band of feathers on the back of their neck and blush pink chest feathers. I think I prefer the underdogs of the bird world!

CAPTIVATING CORVIDS

Corvids belong to a family of birds called corvidae (sometimes they are collectively called 'crows') and are considered some of the cleverest birds on the planet. They include crows, ravens, rooks, jays, magpies, choughs, treepies and nutcrackers. There are 133 species around the world, but we have eight special species of corvid in the UK and Ireland, and they are some of my favourite and most fascinating birds. Aesop's fable, 'The Thirsty Crow', told the tale of a clever crow who dropped stones into a tall jar, or hydria, raising the water level to quench its thirst. This may seem like a tale of fiction, but it is very close to the truth. They can sequence and solve complex problems, use tools such as sticks to acquire food, and can even recognise individual faces. If a particular human has threatened a corvid in the past, they remember them and are very aggressively vocal if they return! I think that corvids possess an intelligence that deserves our respect and admiration.

To find a jay feather is to find treasure, to be met by a raven high on a mountain top is like a message from the gods, to see a roosting of rooks is to remember that community and friends are important, to see a chough is to be met by royalty, to see a a magpie, well, that can mean all sorts of things! Let me introduce you to our charismatic and captivating corvids:

JAY

Forest planter and dweller, the jay is the most colourful of all our corvids. They hide acorns, many of which grow into oak trees. Jays have a very clever way of preventing parasites on their feathers: they enter a wood ant nest and trigger the defensive release of formic acid from the angry ants. It acts as a powerful insecticide, keeping the jay healthy and maintained.

RAVEN

The raven is most mystical of all corvids, found high in the hills and mountains. In Norse mythology the god Odin had two ravens called Huginn (which means 'thought') and Muninn ('memory'). Vikings had ravens on their armour, helmets and longships to invoke the power of Odin in battle.

CARRION CROW

They appear as black as night, but if you look closely, the carrion crow dazzles with green and purple. They were often seen as bad omens as they eat flesh, just like a bird of prey. This may seem a little macabre, but it's just nature, and in the wild, they and other meat-eating animals clean up dead matter, which is very important.

CHOUGH (CHUFF)

Magical cliff dweller. In myth and legend, King Arthur is said to have transformed into a chough after his death. They are very tame around humans and forage amidst them, using their curved bill to dig for insects.

MAGPIE

Monochrome, in its shiny suit, the magpie is unmistakable. Seen as harbingers of luck, they have a rhyme all to themselves.

*One for sorrow, two for joy.
Three for a girl, four for a boy.
Five for silver, six for gold.
Seven for a secret never told.
Eight for a wish, nine for a kiss.
Ten for a bird you must not miss.*

JACKDAW

With their beautiful white irises and ash-grey nape, jackdaws are the smallest native member of the corvid family. They love to chatter amongst themselves and are highly social. If they find a good feeding spot, they tell other jackdaws: they are extremely clever.

ROOK

Grey-beaked, with a greyish-white featherless area around its face, the rook's feathers are silky soft. Seeing a parliament of rooks roosting at dusk is something I find truly wonderful. They are mesmerising to watch.

HOODED CROW

Silver and black, hooded crows have similar diets to the carrion crow, but they are much more sociable birds and interact in large groups. In Finland, hooded crows have been observed swooping down and pulling in fishing rods situated in ice holes to eat the fish. Extraordinary!

FEED THE BIRDS

During the summer months birds will still visit your garden, so do fill up your feeders with sunflower hearts – the majority of garden birds love these – but the best solution is to provide wild plants, which in their flowering stage will also benefit pollinators.

I know it's not always possible to plant native trees and shrubs such as ROWAN, HAWTHORN and HOLLY, which provide much-needed berries in the colder months, but there are easy alternatives to try, such as sunflowers! All our garden birds love eating high energy seeds from these easy-to-grow bursts of sunshine.

Found in most gardens, DANDELIONS make great food for birds once they have reached their fairy clock stage. BULLFINCHES especially love them, and I have seen them eating DAISIES too. Planting TEASELS from seed, so easy to grow, will also attract insects, and in late summer, just watch a charm of GOLDFINCHES alight on the seed heads to feed in a garrulous, glorious feast! If you have ivy growing in your garden, know that this is such a brilliant plant for wildlife. The flowers nourish BEES and HOVERFLIES during autumn, before they hibernate, and and the berries are a fantastic food for birds during winter. IVY also provides little havens for birds to disappear into as it provides excellent cover from predators. ROSES also provide birds with a brilliant supply of hips and berries, and HONEYSUCKLE attracts a wide number of insects, which benefit birds too.

A NOTE ON CLEANING BIRD FEEDERS

We all love garden birds visiting our homes and we take great joy in observing and feeding them. In order to keep them safe and free from disease, it's crucially important to keep our feeding stations squeaky clean. Can you imagine eating your dinner from a plate you never clean? Yuk! Unlike grass, trees and hedgerows, plastic and metal pick up a lot of dirt, rust, droppings and residue. Here are a few tips to protect your garden birds:

1. Clean your feeders outside with warm water, a weak disinfectant and a separate bottle brush. Make it part of your regular routine.

2. If food hasn't been eaten in a few days to a week, reduce the amount of food you are giving, to prevent mould.

3. Move your feeders monthly to prevent a build-up of bird poo. If this isn't possible, dispose of any foliage underneath.

4. Wash your water bowls daily, and make sure they are nice and dry before adding fresh water.

SCIENTISTS GIVE ALL LIVING THINGS LATIN NAMES SO THEY CAN BE RECOGNISED ALL AROUND THE WORLD, REGARDLESS OF LANGUAGE. HERE ARE ALL THE LATIN BIRD NAMES IN YOUR BOOK OF BIRDS!

Archaeopteryx

Avocet
Recurvirostra

Barn Owl
Tyto alba

Barnacle Goose
Branta leucopsis

Bewick's Swan
Cygnus bewickii

Black-Headed Gull
Chroicocephalus ridibundus

Blackbird (Eurasian)
Turdus merula

Blackcap (Eurasian)
Sylvia atricapilla

Blue Tit (Eurasian)
Cyanistes caeruleus

Brambling
Fringilla montifringilla

Brent Goose (Light-Bellied)
Branta bernicla hrota

Bullfinch (Eurasian)
Pyrrhula pyrrhula

Buzzard (common)
Buteo buteo

Carrion Crow
Corvus corone

Chaffinch
Fringilla coelebs

Chiffchaff
Phylloscopus collybita

Chough
Pyrrhocorax pyrrhocorax

Coal Tit
Periparus ater

Crossbill
Loxia

Crow
Corvus

Cuckoo (common)
Cuculus canorus

Curlew (Eurasian)
Numenius arquata

Dunnock
Prunella modularis

Fieldfare
Turdus pilaris

Goldfinch
Carduelis carduelis

Great Crested Grebe
Podiceps cristatus

Great Tit
Parus major

Greenfinch
Chloris chloris

Grey Heron
Ardea cinerea

Guillemot
Uria aalge

Hawfinch
Coccothraustes coccothraustes

Hen Harrier
Circus cyaneus

Hooded Crow
Corvus cornix

House Martin
Delichon urbicum

Hummingbird
Trochilidae

Jackdaw (Eurasian)
Coloeus monedula

Jay (Eurasian)
Garrulus glandarius

Kestrel
Falco tinnunculus

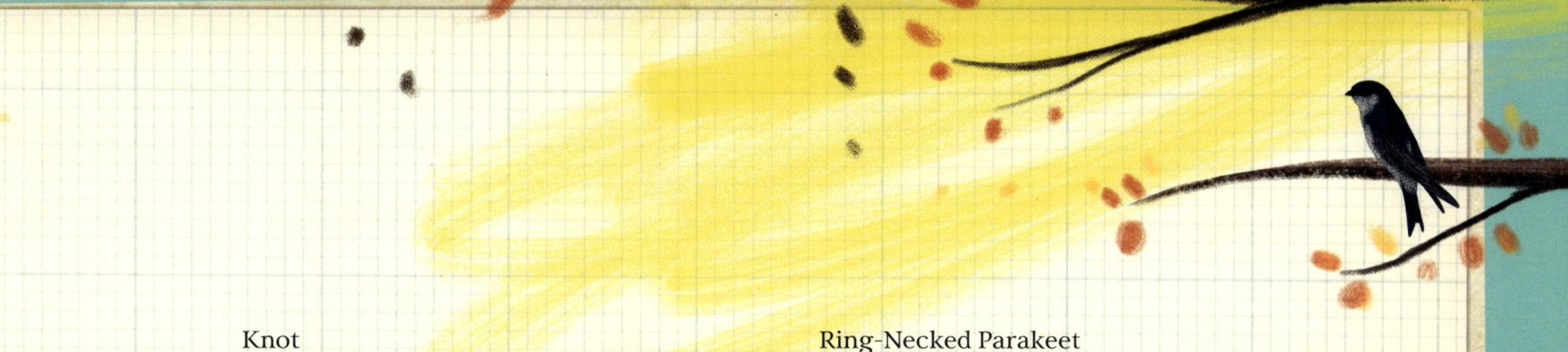

Knot
Calidris canutus

Little Egret
Egretta garzetta

Long-Tailed Tit
Aegithalos caudatus

Magpie (Eurasian)
Pica pica

Mallard Duck
Anas platyrhynchos

Mistle Thrush
Turdus viscivorus

Moorhen
Gallinula chloropus

Mute Swan
Cygnus olor

Nightingale
Luscinia megarhynchos

Nutcracker
Nucifraga

Ostrich
Struthio

Peregrine Falcon
Falco peregrinus

Pigeon (Rock Dove/Feral Pigeon)
Columba livia

Pink-Footed Goose
Anser brachyrhynchus

Pochard
Aythya ferina

Raven
Corvus corax

Red Kite
Milvus milvus

Redpoll
Acanthis flammea

Redwing
Turdus iliacus

Ring-Necked Parakeet
Psittacula krameri

Ringed Plover
Charadrius hiaticula

Robin (Eurasian)
Erithacus rubecula

Rook
Corvus frugilegus

Siskin (Eurasian)
Carduelis spinus

Skylark (Eurasian)
Alauda arvensis

Snipe
Gallinago gallinago

Song Thrush
Turdus philomelos

Sparrow (house)
Passer domesticus

Starling
Sturnus vulgaris

Swallow
Hirundo rustica

Swift
Apus apus

Teal
Anas crecca

Tern
Sternidae

Treepie
Crypsirininae

Turnstone
Arenaria interpres

Twite
Carduelis flavirostris

Waxwing
Bombycilla

GLOSSARY

Adaptation
The way that an animal or plant has changed so it is better suited to life in its environment.

Ancestor
An earlier type of animal or plant from which today's generations are descended.

Asymmetric
Two parts of something which are not the same.

Avian
Relating to birds.

Binocular vision
The way the brain uses the vision from two eyes to help judge distance.

Bird hide
A camouflaged shelter from which a person can watch birds nearby.

Brood
A family group of eggs or chicks that were laid at the same time.

Camouflage
Colours and patterns that help an animal to hide.

Catkin
A flowering spike that hangs from trees such as willow and hazel.

Charm
A group of goldfinches.

Climate change
The way that the world's climate is changing. Today, this is happening because of the damage done to the atmosphere by carbon dioxide and other forms of pollution.

Clutch
A group of eggs that are all laid at the same time.

Conservation
The protection and preservation of the natural environment and wildlife.

Crustacean
An animal with four or more pairs of limbs and a tough outer skin. Shrimps, woodlice and crabs are all crustaceans.

Cygnet
A young swan.

Ecologist
A person who studies ecology – the way that living things are all related to each other and their surroundings.

Environment
The surroundings in which a living thing exists.

Estuary
The area where a river opens out into the sea.

Evolve

Animals and plants that evolve are changing over time, to survive in an ever-changing world.

Extinct

When a species of living thing is extinct it has gone for ever.

Fledgling

A young bird that is able to fly.

Flock

A group of birds.

Foliage

The leaves on a plant.

Follicle

A part of the skin from which a hair or a feather grows.

Forage

To search for food.

Fungi

Living things, such as mushrooms and toadstools, that produce spores and feed on living or dead matter.

Habitat

The place where an animal, plant or fungus lives.

Hibernate

To spend the winter in a dormant, or resting, state.

Hormone

A special chemical made by the body and transported in blood. A hormone brings about a change in an animal or plant.

Insecticide

A chemical that kills insects.

Insulate

To trap heat close to the body.

Keratin

A type of tough protein that is found in hair, nails, claws, beaks and feathers.

Meadow

A large area, or field, of grassland.

Migration

A long journey that animals go on to find resources, such as food or water.

Mollusc

A type of soft-bodied animal that may be protected by a shell. Snails, slugs and shellfish are all molluscs.

Moor

A large area of open, wild land that is often covered in low-growing plants such as heather.

Moult

To shed old feathers.

Naturalist

A person who studies, and is interested in, the natural world.

Nocturnal

Most active at night.

Nutrients

The chemicals in food that help living things to grow and stay healthy.

Ornithology

The study of birds.

Parasite

A living thing that lives in, or on, another living thing and does it harm.

Plumage

A bird's feathers.

Pollinator

An animal, such as an insect, bat or bird, which transfers pollen between flowers.

Predator

An animal that hunts other animals to eat.

Prey

An animal that is hunted by other animals.

Raptor

A bird of prey.

Reptile

An animal with a backbone and scaly skin, such as snakes and lizards.

Roost

A place where birds settle to rest, especially at night.

Scavenge

To look for dead animals to eat.

Species

A kind, or sort, of living thing. Animals of one species can only reproduce with animals of the same species.

Syrinx

The part of a bird's body where sound is made.

Talons

The claws on a bird's feet, especially a bird of prey.

Territory

The area that an animal protects and defends from other animals.

Ultraviolet

A type of light that humans cannot see, but many animals can.

Vole

A small, furry mouse-like animal with a rounded snout.

HELPFUL ORGANISATIONS

Birdwatch Ireland www.birdwatchireland.ie
Irish Wildlife Trust www.iwt.ie
BTO – British Trust for Ornithology www.bto.org
National Trust www.nationaltrust.org.uk
National Trust for Scotland www.nts.org.uk
The Rivers Trust www.theriverstrust.org
RSPB – Royal Society for the Protection of Birds www.rspb.org.uk
The Wildlife Trusts www.wildlifetrusts.org
Wildlife Watch www.wildlifewatch.org.uk

DARA McANULTY is an award-winning author, naturalist and activist from Northern Ireland. He's received many awards for his conservation work, including from BBC *Springwatch*, *The Daily Mirror* and *Birdwatch* magazine. Dara is the youngest ever recipient of the RSPB medal for conservation. He lives with his family and Rosie the rescue greyhound at the foot of the Mourne Mountains in County Down.

BARRY FALLS grew up in rural Northern Ireland, where he spent a lot of time drawing pictures and writing stories to go with them. He is a commercial illustrator, who has received multiple awards for his work with clients such as *The New York Times*, *American Airlines* and *The Telegraph*.